EXPLORING THE HUMAN BODY

The Brain and Nervous System

Carol Ballard

FRANKLIN WATTS
LONDON•SYDNEY

First published in 2005 by
Franklin Watts
96 Leonard Street
London EC2A 4XD

Franklin Watts Australia
Level 17/207 Kent Street
Sydney NSW 2000

Produced by Arcturus Publishing Ltd,
26/27 Bickels Yard, 151–153 Bermondsey Street, London SE1 3HA

Series concept: Alex Woolf
Editor: Alex Woolf
Designer: Peta Morey
Artwork: Michael Courtney
Picture researcher: Glass Onion Pictures
Consultant: Dr Kristina Routh

Picture Credits
Science Photo Library: 4 (TEK Image), 6 (Alfred Pasieka), 9 (Colin Cuthbert),
11 (Martin Riedl), 15 (BSIP, Barouillet), 18 (Renée Lynn), 21 (Martin Riedl),
22 (Sheila Terry), 24 (Oscar Burriel), 26 (Oscar Burriel), 29 (David Constantine).
Topfoto: 16 (Ellen Senisi / The Image Works).

Every attempt has been made to clear copyright. Should there be any
inadvertent omission, please apply to the publisher for rectification.

A CIP catalogue record for this book is available from the British Library

ISBN 0 7496 5963 7

Printed in Singapore

T22238

Contents

What are the Brain and Nerves?

Your brain is your body's control centre. It monitors and controls everything that your body does every minute of every day. Even when you are fast asleep, your brain is still working, maintaining vital processes like your heartbeat and breathing.

Your brain controls your muscles, allowing you to move your whole body when you run and jump, and to make smaller movements like licking an ice-cream and wiggling your toes.

All your thoughts and ideas, feelings and emotions are possible because of your brain. It allows you to learn and remember, to puzzle out problems and to ask questions. It lets you dream and imagine, and have new and original ideas.

Your brain is connected to every part of your body by nerves. Your sense organs, like your eyes and ears, collect information from the world around you. Nerves carry this information to the brain. Your brain sends messages to other parts of your body, such as muscles, via the nerves. Together, your brain, nerves and sense organs make up your nervous system.

The spinal cord, an important bundle of nerves, is the main route through which information passes between the brain and the body. For example, if you stand in a puddle, a message will travel from your foot to your brain via the spinal cord. If your brain thinks standing in a

Your brain is where all your thoughts and ideas are formed and stored.

puddle is a bad idea, a message will travel from your brain to your muscles to make them move your foot.

If your brain or spinal cord is injured, you may have difficulty moving or thinking properly. Therefore it is important for them to be carefully protected. The strong bones of your skull protect your brain, and the bony column of your backbone protects your spinal cord.

This diagram shows the brain and nervous system in the human body.

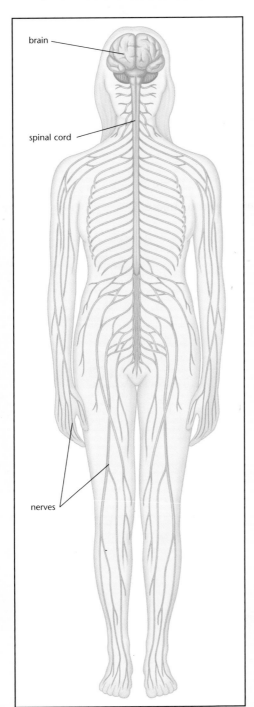

brain

spinal cord

nerves

Case notes

Why should I wear a safety helmet?

If you wanted to carry an egg home from the shops, it would be safer in an egg box than loose in a carrier bag, wouldn't it? The shell protects the delicate egg inside, but some knocks and bangs are just too much for it. Your head is like this too – your skull bones protect the delicate brain inside, but hard knocks can damage the bones themselves. Wearing a safety helmet gives your head extra protection, just as the egg box provides protection for the egg – so it makes sense to wear a safety helmet for sports like cricket, horse riding, skateboarding and cycling.

Inside the Brain

Your brain is a pinkish-grey organ that sits inside your skull. It is wrinkled and feels a bit like a stiff jelly. It is about the size of a small cauliflower and takes up most of the space inside the top and back parts of your head. An adult's brain weighs about 1,300 to 1,400 grams and contains more than 100,000,000,000 (one hundred thousand million) nerve cells!

The bones of the skull form an outer protective layer for the brain. The brain itself is wrapped inside three thin layers called meninges. The spaces between the brain and the meninges contain a liquid called cerebrospinal fluid, or CSF. This acts as a cushion to stop the brain banging against the bones.

The brain has four main parts, called the cerebrum, cerebellum, diencephalon and brainstem. Each part has its own special job to do.

The cerebrum is the part of the brain that we use when we think and it makes up nearly nine tenths of the brain. The cerebrum is divided into two halves, called the left and right cerebral hemispheres. There is a deep groove between them, but they are joined by a narrow "bridge" that carries messages between them.

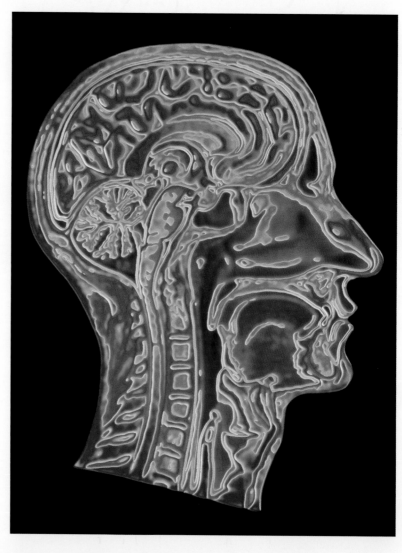

This image of the brain was taken using a modern hospital scanner.

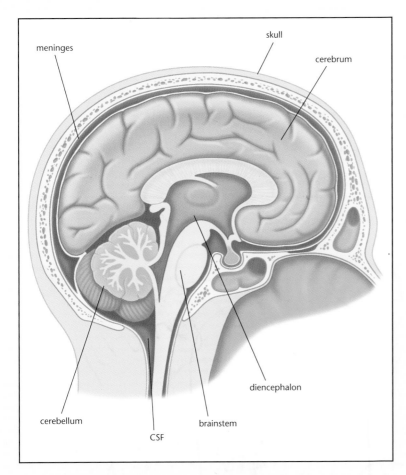

meninges

skull

cerebrum

cerebellum

CSF

brainstem

diencephalon

This diagram shows the main parts of the brain.

The **cerebellum** makes up about one tenth of the brain. It sits below the cerebrum, at the back of the head. It is involved with helping us to maintain our balance and posture. It also allows us to make smooth, co-ordinated movements instead of stiff, jerky movements.

The **diencephalon** is in the centre of the brain. It helps to control how alert you feel and is responsible for basic feelings such as anger and fear, hunger and thirst. It is also involved in handling information coming into the brain from sense organs like your eyes and ears.

The **brainstem** is the lowest part of the brain. Its lower end passes through a hole in the base of the skull and continues down as the spinal cord. It handles all the automatic brain functions, controlling vital processes such as heartbeat, breathing and digestion.

Case notes

How does blood get to the brain?

Like every other part of the body, the brain needs a blood supply to bring fresh oxygen and nutrients and to take away waste products. Two arteries take blood from the heart to the upper and front parts of the brain and two more arteries take blood to the back of the brain. Blood is carried around the brain through a network of smaller blood vessels. It flows back to the heart through two main veins.

Brain Map

Most of our thinking takes place within the cerebral cortex – the outer layers of the cerebrum. The surface of the cerebral cortex is wrinkled, with lots of bumps and grooves, which make it look rather like a walnut! Because it is folded up on itself like this, it has a large surface. This means that it can contain a lot more brain tissue than it could if it were smooth and flat.

The cerebral cortex has three types of area:

- sensory areas, which receive signals from the rest of the body;
- motor areas, which send signals to the rest of the body;
- association areas, which sort out all the incoming information, make sense of it and decide what needs to be done.

This diagram shows that different jobs are carried out in different parts of the brain.

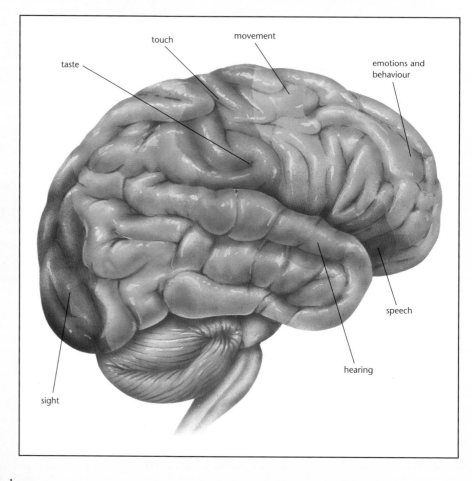

taste — touch — movement — emotions and behaviour — speech — hearing — sight

At the front of the cerebral cortex, behind the forehead, is an area that controls emotions and feelings and determines some of the ways in which we behave. The motor area that controls speech is here, as well as another motor area that controls most of our other movements.

This therapist (right) is helping a stroke patient to learn to speak again.

Behind this, at the top of the cerebral cortex, is a sensory area that receives signals from skin, muscles, joints and body organs. Information from all over the body is sorted out here, and then passed on to other parts of the brain for action to be taken. This area of the cerebral cortex also controls your senses of taste and touch.

At the sides of the cerebral cortex are the sensory areas that receive signals from the ears. The hearing association areas are here too. These areas control your sense of hearing and are involved in helping you to keep your balance.

The very back part of the cerebral cortex contains the sensory areas that receive signals from your eyes. The sight association areas are also here, and together these areas control your sense of sight.

The innermost part of the cerebral cortex is involved with your sense of smell, and also with your memories.

Case notes

What happens when someone has a 'stroke'?

The brain needs a constant blood supply. If the blood flow to any part of the brain is interrupted, that part may be damaged and unable to work properly. This is called a stroke. It can cause a variety of effects, depending on the part of the brain affected. For example, damage to a motor area may prevent a patient from moving part of his or her body. If the speech area is damaged, the patient may not be able to speak properly. Damage to an association area may make it difficult for a patient to recognize a friend's face. Sometimes the effects are permanent, but in many cases the patient gradually recovers.

Left Brain, Right Brain

The cerebrum is made up from two parts, the left and right hemispheres. Nerves link each hemisphere to the opposite side of the body. This means that the left hemisphere controls the right side of the body, and the right hemisphere controls the left side of the body. Each hemisphere controls a different range of functions and activities.

In about nine out of ten people, the left hemisphere controls activities like speaking, reading and writing. It deals with numbers and calculations and works out logical solutions to problems. So when you are chatting to a friend, writing a report, doing some maths, or playing chess, your left hemisphere is really working hard.

In about nine out of ten people, the right hemisphere controls activities that involve dealing with shapes and colours, distances and positions. It deals with artistic and creative activities. So when you are painting a picture, sketching, designing a pattern or playing a musical instrument, your right hemisphere is doing most of the work.

The left hemisphere works on small details of each task one at a time, while the right hemisphere works on the

These pictures show the functions controlled by each side of the brain.

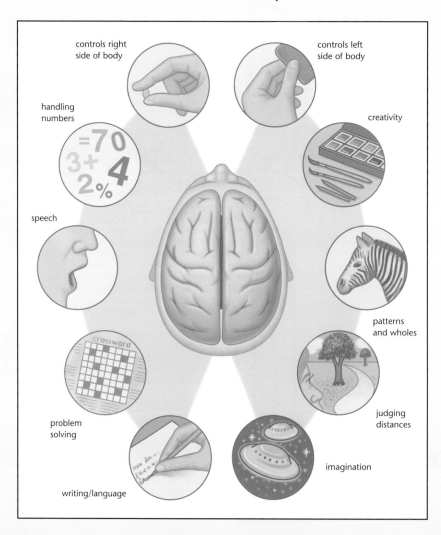

controls right side of body

handling numbers

speech

problem solving

writing/language

controls left side of body

creativity

patterns and wholes

judging distances

imagination

The right hemisphere controls creative activities like painting.

Case notes

What happens if I'm left-handed?

If you are left-handed, you are probably more comfortable using your left hand than your right for jobs such as writing, painting or throwing a ball. You might be left-footed too, and kick a ball with your left foot. This does not mean there is anything different about your brain. In most societies, about one person in ten is left-handed. Among groups of creative people, though, there are usually many more left-handed people than this. Some very famous creative people, such as Leonardo da Vinci, Michelangelo, Mozart and Beethoven, were left-handed. Some people can use either hand equally well for all tasks and are said to be ambidextrous.

whole idea. By working together, they allow you to tackle just about anything you want to!

When a child is very young, both hemispheres work in the same way as each other. During the first seven or eight years of life, one hemisphere (usually the left) gradually becomes more dominant.

For most tasks, the ways in which the hemispheres work are established in childhood and do not change. The links and connections within our brains are formed and determine how good we may be at doing things such as making music, number work, painting or using languages – although how good we actually turn out to be at these things depends on how hard we try.

Linking the Brain and Body

In order for your brain and body to work together, they have to be connected. These connections are formed by the nerves.

Nerves are made up from nerve cells, which each have three main parts:

- a cell body, which is the cell's control centre;
- fine threads (dendrites) that branch out from the cell body, carrying signals from other nerve cells to the cell body;
- a long thin fibre (axon) that carries signals away from the cell body to other nerve cells.

Although the ends of nerve cells may be very close, there are tiny gaps between them called synapses. Chemicals called neurotransmitters carry signals across these gaps.

Nerve cells are packed together in bundles inside a protective layer. These bundles are then arranged to make a larger bundle, with an outer layer to keep it all together. This is a nerve. Some nerves are very thick and contain many thousands of nerve fibres. Others may have only a few.

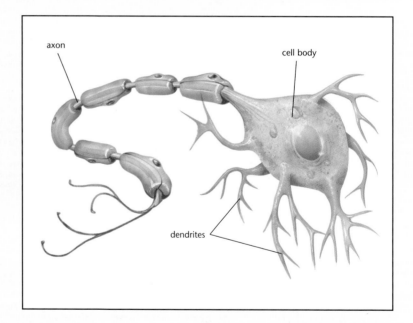

axon

cell body

dendrites

Here you can see the three main parts of a nerve cell.

Cranial Nerves

Twelve pairs of cranial nerves link the brain directly to other parts of the body. Most of the cranial nerves link the brain with parts of the head, including the eyes, ears, nose and tongue. The biggest cranial nerve, called the vagus nerve, links the brain with important organs including the heart, lungs, stomach, intestines, liver and kidneys.

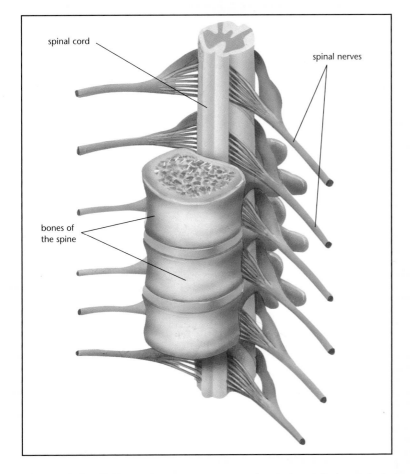

spinal cord

spinal nerves

bones of the spine

Here you can see how the bones of the spine fit around the spinal cord and spinal nerves.

Spinal Cord

The spinal cord connects the brain to the rest of the body. It lies inside the spinal canal, a tunnel made by the bones of the spine. The top end of the spinal cord is joined to the brain at the brainstem. Spinal nerves branch out from the spinal cord at intervals all along its length, linking it to the upper body. The spinal cord ends at about waist-level. From its lower end, more spinal nerves run down inside the spinal canal, connecting the spinal cord to the lower body.

The spinal nerves branch again and again, becoming narrower each time. The very finest branches are linked to sense organs or to special sites within muscles.

Sensing the World

Humans have five senses: sight, hearing, touch, taste and smell. These enable us to find out about the world around us.

Each sense relies on a sense organ to collect information and send it to the brain. Our eyes collect light information and our ears collect sound information. Receptors in our skin collect information about temperature and pressure. Our tongues and noses collect information about chemicals in our food and drink and in the air around us.

When a sense organ is stimulated by its own type of information, it responds by sending out an electrical signal. This travels along a nerve to the appropriate sensory area of the brain. The sensory area and association area then work together to make sense of the information and interpret it.

Sight

When light enters the eye, an image is formed on the inside layer, or retina, of the eye. The retina is sensitive to light and it responds by sending signals along the optic nerve to the sight sensory area in the brain. The sight sensory and association areas work together to interpret

The brain receives a signal when light enters our eyes.

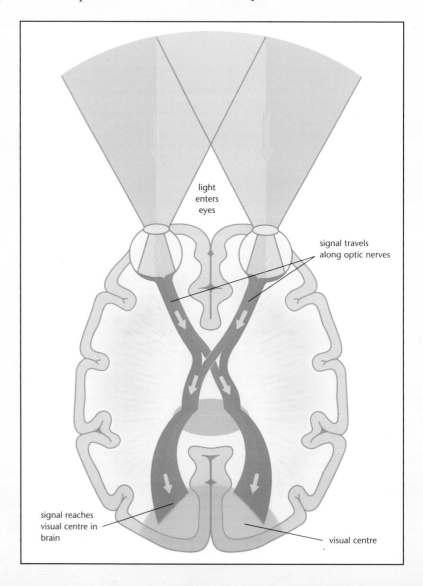

light enters eyes

signal travels along optic nerves

signal reaches visual centre in brain

visual centre

the information and work out what you are seeing. Because your two eyes each get a slightly different view, your brain can work out a three-dimensional image.

Hearing

When sound waves reach the ear, they make internal parts of the ear vibrate. The ear responds by sending signals to the brain along the auditory nerve to the hearing sensory area in the brain. The hearing sensory and association areas work together to interpret the information and work out what you are hearing. Because your two ears are on opposite sides of your head, your brain can pinpoint exactly where the sound came from.

Nerve endings in the skin detect the silky softness of the cat's fur and send a signal to the brain.

Touch

Nerve endings in the skin respond to light touch, pressure, heat, cold, vibration and chemicals. There are several different types of nerve endings, each of which only responds to one type of stimulus. When a nerve ending detects its own special stimulus it responds by sending a signal to the touch sensory area of the brain. The brain then works out what you have felt and where you felt it.

Case notes

Taste and Smell

Taste buds in the surface of the tongue detect chemicals in your food and drink. Receptors in the lining of the nose detect chemicals in the air. When you eat or drink, and when air wafts past your nose, signals are sent to the brain. The brain then works out what you have tasted or smelt. Your ability to taste food is the result of a complicated mixture of signals from both tongue and nose.

Movement

Humans can make large movements such as jumping and somersaulting. We can also make small movements, such as blinking our eyelids or tapping our fingers. Every movement, big or small, is controlled by the brain and nerves.

When you decide you want to make a movement, the motor areas of the cerebral cortex send signals to muscles via motor nerves. These signals make the muscles contract, which moves part of the body. Most muscles move bones, but some move other parts; for example, muscles in your face move skin.

If this was all that happened, your movements would be stiff and jerky, like a robot toy. Your brain uses a system of constant checks to help you move smoothly. This system also helps you to remember particular sequences of movements; the more you practise a movement, the easier it becomes, as your brain remembers it and refines it a little more every time you repeat it.

This checking system involves the cerebellum, which is linked by nerves to the diencephalon, the spinal cord and the body muscles. When the motor area of the cerebral cortex sends signals to the muscles, it also sends signals to the cerebellum. When a muscle starts to contract, tiny receptors in the muscles and joints send signals back to the cerebellum. Sending information back like this is called feedback. It allows the cerebellum to monitor the movement and to check it against the original instruction from the cerebral cortex.

As you repeat particular movements, such as playing a chord on a guitar, the cerebellum learns and refines them.

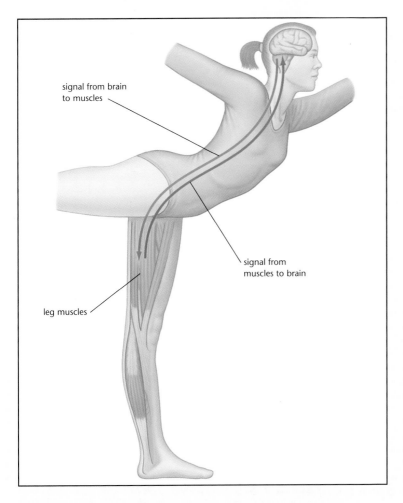

signal from brain
to muscles

signal from
muscles to brain

leg muscles

This diagram shows the feedback
system that helps us to co-ordinate
our movements.

The cerebellum corrects any differences or problems.
Because it does this on its own, without involving the
cerebral cortex (the "thinking" part of the brain), you can
make a movement without actually having to think about
it. The cerebellum remembers the movements and so you
become more skilled at performing them.

For example, a toddler does not know precisely which
muscles to move and how to co-ordinate the movements in
order to pick up a pencil and make a mark. By
experimenting and trying again and again, he or she
gradually finds this out. With practice, the child's drawing
and writing skills improve. The cerebellum has learned and
remembered precisely what to do. The same sort of
feedback system is involved whenever we develop a new
skill such as playing a musical instrument, hitting a
rounders ball or learning a dance step.

Case notes

How do we balance?

The feedback from receptors
around the body to the
cerebellum also helps you to
maintain your posture and
balance. The cerebellum
keeps checking the exact
position of every part of your
body, keeping you upright
and preventing you from
falling over.

Monitoring and Controlling

The brain and nervous system are vitally important in keeping your body alive and functioning properly. A continuous system of monitoring and controlling goes on without you being aware of it. The parts of the brain and nervous system involved in this are called the autonomic nervous system, or ANS.

Just about everything that goes on in your body is monitored and controlled by the ANS. If you get too hot, the ANS starts cooling processes: it increases sweat production, widens blood capillaries and sends messages to your cerebral cortex to prompt you to take action such as having a cold drink. If you get too cold, the ANS does the opposite: it decreases sweat production, narrows capillaries and sends signals to the cerebral cortex to prompt you to put on a jumper. The ANS also controls:

- how fast your heart beats;
- how quickly you breathe in and out;
- the movement of food through your digestive system;
- production of body fluids such as sweat, tears and saliva;
- the levels of substances such as sugar, water and minerals in your blood;
- removal of waste products by your kidneys.

The ANS helps your body to cool down after exercise.

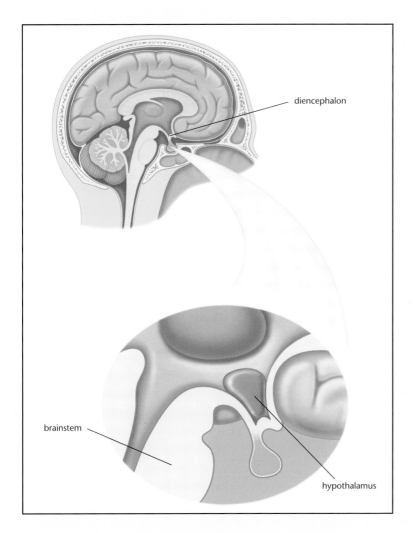

diencephalon

brainstem

hypothalamus

Here you can see where the hypothalamus lies deep inside the brain.

The ANS is mainly controlled by the hypothalamus, a tiny part of the diencephalon deep inside the brain.

The ANS has two parts, the sympathetic system and the parasympathetic system. These work in opposite ways, rather like the accelerator and brakes in a car: the sympathetic system speeds things up, and the parasympathetic system slows them down. For example, the sympathetic system makes your heart beat faster when you exercise, and the parasympathetic system slows it down when you rest. Most of the time, the two work together and their effects are perfectly balanced. They maintain your body in a stable state called homeostasis. If something happens to upset homeostasis, one system will take over, taking action to stabilize everything and bring the body back to its normal state.

Case notes

What is the body clock?

A small area of the hypothalamus is called the body clock. It receives signals from the eyes, telling it how much daylight there is. The body clock works on a twenty-four-hour cycle, maintaining the body's daily patterns, or biorhythms. These affect when we feel alert or sleepy, as well as other processes such as changes in body temperature, production of urine and repair of injuries. If anything happens to upset the body clock's cycle, we can feel tired and lethargic. Many people suffer from "jet lag" after a long flight – this is because it takes their body clock a while to alter its cycle and adjust to the new time.

Memory and Learning

Exactly how our brains store our memories, and how we learn, are still mysteries to doctors and scientists. Although we know something about the areas of the brain that are involved, nobody has yet worked out the precise mechanisms that take place.

The cerebral cortex is the area of the brain that allows us to think. Somehow, information passes from the cerebral cortex to other areas where it can be stored. This information storage is called memory. There is no single place in the brain where memories are stored. Instead, scientists think that memories are stored as connections between millions of nerve cells in many different parts of the brain.

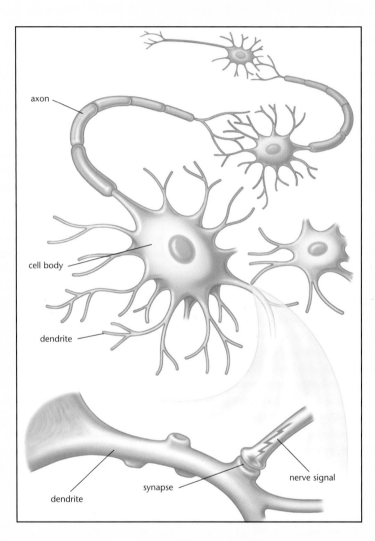

This diagram shows links between nerve cells.

Short-Term Memory

There are some things that you only need to remember for a short time. Your brain stores the information for as long as you need it and then forgets it. For example, if you look up a telephone number, you might remember it for long enough to dial the number but will probably have forgotten it by the time you have finished making the call. This is called short-term memory.

Long-Term Memory

Information from short-term memory can be transferred into long-term memory. This is a more permanent memory that allows you to store memories for days, months and years. For example, you can probably recite your home address and telephone number – this is because they are stored as long-term memories.

Learning

When you look at words in a book, signals are sent from your eyes to your brain. Nerve cells in the brain are activated and the brain makes sense of what you see. If you read the words over and over again, the same nerve cells are activated again and again and connections between them are made. A similar process happens when you listen repeatedly to something, or repeat an action many times. This allows us to learn things and remember them.

The more we repeat something, the stronger and more firmly established the connections within the brain become. If we do not do something for a long time, the connections eventually weaken and we lose the memory – we forget.

When we learn, new connections form within the brain.

Case notes

What is dyslexia?

Dyslexia is a condition that affects the ability to read, write and spell. It is often also linked to short-term memory problems, making it difficult to remember lists and sequences. People with dyslexia are as intelligent as anybody else, but find traditional learning activities very difficult. They can be taught special ways of dealing with the problems dyslexia causes. This enables them to do well at school and be successful in whatever career they choose.

Sleep and Dreams

You may be asleep, but your brain has to keep on working! It controls basic body processes such as your heartbeat and breathing, just as it does when you are awake.

Why Do We Sleep?

Doctors and scientists do not know exactly why we sleep, but they do know that sleep is vital to us – amazingly, lack of sleep will cause death more quickly than lack of food! Going to sleep may be the body's way of saving energy. While we sleep, repair processes continue, helping the body to recover from any damage that has occurred during the day.

Sleep Patterns

By using a machine to monitor and record brainwaves, scientists have found that our sleep is made up of several different stages:

Sleep gives our bodies a chance to rest, repair themselves and be ready for the next day.

Stage 1 sleep: In the first few minutes of sleep, the heartbeat and breathing rate slow down and muscles relax. The brain is very busy at this stage. People often feel as if they are very light or floating.

Stage 2 sleep: There are sudden bursts of brain activity in this stage.

Stage 3 sleep: This is deep sleep. The body temperature drops and brainwaves become larger and slower.

Stage 4 sleep: This is the deepest sleep stage. Heart and breathing rates drop even more and brainwaves become even longer and slower. People who sleepwalk are usually in stage 4 sleep.

REM sleep: in this stage, the heart and breathing rates speed up and muscles twitch. Brainwaves become faster and more irregular. Although the eyelids stay closed, the eyes move quickly to and fro, giving this stage its name of rapid eye movement (REM) sleep. REM sleep occurs just before another spell of stage 1 sleep.

A typical night's sleep contains several sleep cycles as we move from one sleep stage to the next and back again.

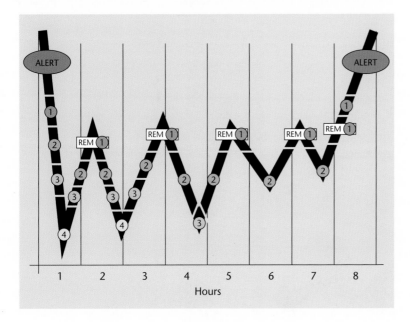

Here you can see the sleep patterns for a typical night.

Dreams and REM Sleep

Dreams occur during REM sleep. We only remember our dreams if we wake up very soon after the end of a period of REM sleep. Nobody knows exactly what dreams are or why we have them. The areas of the brain involved in memory and learning are active during REM sleep. This suggests that REM sleep is important in sorting memories and learning from the previous day.

Feelings and Emotions

We experience a variety of feelings and emotions every day. Some are pleasant, like love and happiness; others are unpleasant, like fear and sadness. Your brain plays an important part in the emotions you experience and in the way you react to them.

Your sense organs are constantly sending signals to your brain, carrying information about the world around you. Your brain works out what you have seen, heard, touched, tasted or smelt. It also draws on your memories to link these sensations with previous experiences. For example, when you see someone coming towards you, your brain links the image of the person to your memories. If the memories associated with that person are good, you experience feelings of pleasure. If the memories are bad, you experience unpleasant feelings.

The most important parts of the brain involved in feelings, emotions and memories are the hypothalamus and thalamus. The limbic system, which lies deep inside the brain, is also involved. It has a direct link with your nose, so smells and memories are closely associated. This is why smells can sometimes trigger powerful memories.

One of the most powerful emotions is fear. If your brain thinks something could hurt you, it prepares your body to either fight or run away. The cerebral cortex sends signals to the hypothalamus, which then sends signals to the adrenal glands that lie close to the kidneys. These release a chemical messenger called adrenaline, which travels around in the blood. Some of the effects of adrenaline include:

- increased heartbeat and breathing rate to send extra oxygen and nutrients to the muscles – you feel your heart hammering and you may start to pant;

All your feelings and emotions are controlled by your brain.

- the muscles are prepared for action – you feel tense and shivery;
- reduced blood flow to the skin to make up for extra going to the muscles – you look pale;
- reduced blood flow to the digestive system to make up for extra going to the muscles – your stomach feels hollow and your mouth feels dry.

This sequence of events is sometimes called an FFF response: you feel Fright so your body prepares to Fight or Flee!

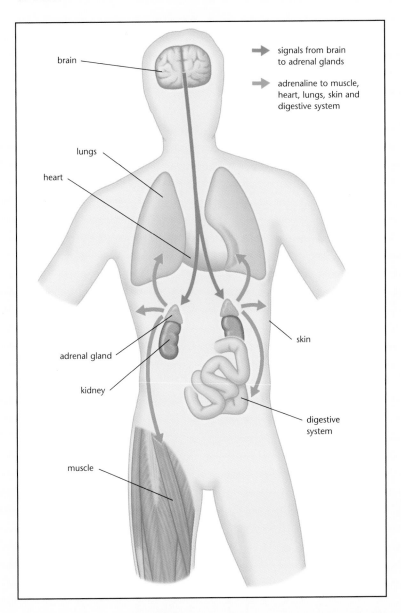

brain

signals from brain
to adrenal glands

adrenaline to muscle,
heart, lungs, skin and
digestive system

lungs

heart

adrenal gland

kidney

skin

digestive
system

muscle

This diagram shows how the brain prepares the body when you are frightened.

Case notes

Why do I get "butterflies" when I'm nervous?

We often feel "butterflies" when we are anxious about something like an exam. This is because your brain interprets your anxiety as fear and mounts an FFF response. This reduces the blood supply to muscles in your digestive system and you feel this as butterflies in your stomach. You cannot control it fully, but sitting quietly and taking a few deep breaths can often help you to feel calmer.

Brain Development

Our brains change and develop throughout our lives. Everything we experience creates new connections between brain cells, and these connections are constantly being updated, reinforced or lost.

The shape of a baby's brain is already formed six months before it is born. At this stage, the surface of the brain is flat and smooth. Its wrinkles and grooves slowly develop during the next few weeks. Scientists think that babies can hear and recognize some sounds before they are born. By the time the baby is born, its brain is fully formed.

Babies

A newborn baby's brain weighs about 350 grams, which is about one quarter of its adult weight. As a baby grows and develops, it slowly begins to find out about its own body and the world around it. The baby begins to remember and recognize familiar people and objects. It learns to communicate and to control its movements. All of these things are made possible by the formation of new connections between nerve cells in the brain.

A baby soon learns to recognize its mother's face and voice.

The First Year

During a baby's first year of life, its brain grows rapidly. By a baby's first birthday, its brain weighs about a thousand grams, which is about two thirds of its adult size. The range of skills that the baby develops during this first year is amazing – at no other time in our lives do we learn so much so quickly.

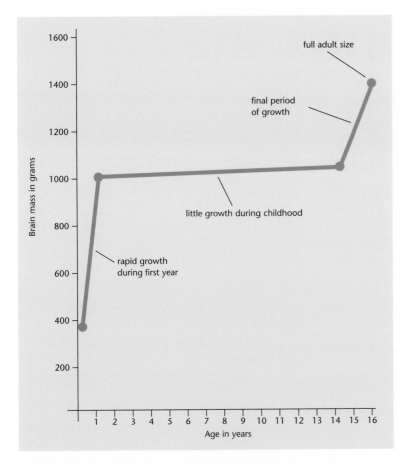

The brain grows rapidly during the first year of life and during the teenage years.

Childhood

The brain grows very little during the childhood years. Most of the changes and developments are internal and are the result of continued learning and experience. Many adults are able to remember some things from when they were very young, with their earliest memories usually being from when they were about three or four years old.

Teenage and Adult Years

Between the ages of fourteen and sixteen, the brain has its last major period of growth. By the end of this time, it will have reached its full adult size. Throughout our adulthood, as we continue to learn and experience new things, new connections are made in our brains and new memories are stored.

Case notes

Why are old people often forgetful?

As a person gets older, connections between some of the cells in his or her brain may break down. If a connection is destroyed, the person can no longer recall the memory – it is lost and forgotten. Strangely, memories from the distant past are often retained while more recent memories are lost. For example, although elderly people may clearly remember events from their childhood, they may forget things that happened to them just the day before.

When Things Go Wrong

Most people have perfectly healthy and well-functioning brains throughout their lives. There are some conditions, though, that can make life very difficult for those who suffer from them.

Meningitis

This is an infection and inflammation of the meninges, the thin layers between the brain and the skull. It can be caused by a virus or bacteria. Viral meningitis is the most common and least serious, often seeming like just a bad dose of flu. Bacterial meningitis can also seem like flu, but in some cases it can be very serious and even fatal. Brain damage can occur as the inflammation increases pressure inside the skull and upsets the chemical balance within the brain. Antibiotics can be used to treat bacterial meningitis and – because it can spread from one person to another – many people are immunized against it.

Epilepsy

In a person with epilepsy, the brain has occasional bursts of electrical activity. Millions of nerve cells in the brain fire random signals at the same time, causing an "overload" in the connections between them. This is called an epileptic

By putting electrodes on the skull, doctors can monitor electrical activity inside the brain.

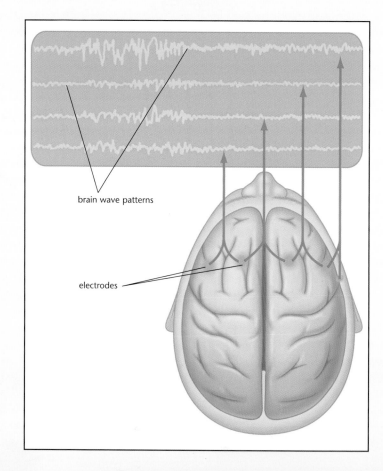

brain wave patterns

electrodes

seizure. Some seizures may cause the person to experience strange smells, sounds and flashes of light. More widespread seizures may involve muscles too, so that a person may fall and make uncontrollable movements. There are several medicines that can be used to treat and control epilepsy.

Concussion

Concussion is the most common brain injury and is usually the result of a blow to the head. It can cause a headache, sleepiness and difficulty in concentrating. Concussion causes a loss of memory that may last just a few seconds – so that the person hardly realizes it has happened – or for several hours. Anybody who has suffered a knock to the head should be watched carefully for a while to make sure that there is no serious injury.

Cerebral Palsy

Cerebral palsy is the result of damage to the brain before birth. It can cause problems with balance, movement, speech, and senses such as sight and hearing. Although some everyday activities may be very difficult for people with cerebral palsy, many sufferers work hard to make the most of their lives despite their physical disabilities.

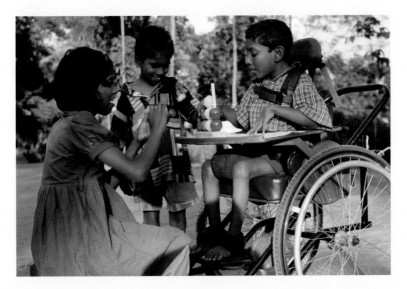

This child with cerebral palsy has a special wheelchair that allows him to move around independently, and play and learn with his friends.

Case notes

What is a headache?

Most people have had a headache at some time. This is often the result of being tired, anxious or stressed. Bad colds, blocked sinuses, toothache and eye strain can also cause headaches. A quiet rest or sleep can often help. Some medicines can be taken to treat headaches but it is better to avoid taking these too often. Only very rarely is a headache caused by a serious problem or illness.

Glossary

adrenaline A hormone (chemical carried in the blood) released in response to fear.

adrenal glands The parts of the body that produce adrenaline.

autonomic nervous system The parts of the brain and nerves that control and monitor your body automatically.

biorhythms Natural body cycles and patterns.

body clock The part of the brain that regulates biorhythms and other cycles.

brainwave An electrical pattern within the brain.

cell One of the tiny units from which all living things are made.

cerebellum The part of the brain involved with movement and co-ordination.

cerebral To do with the brain.

cerebral cortex The outer layers of the cerebrum.

cerebrum The thinking part of the brain.

diencephalon One of the deepest areas of the brain.

hypothalamus The part of the brain involved in automatic responses, memories and emotions.

limbic system A part of the brain involved with memories and emotions.

meninges Thin layers between the skull and brain.

nerve The part of the nervous system that carries signals.

nerve cell A single cell from a nerve or brain.

receptor A nerve ending that detects a stimulus.

reflex A reaction that bypasses the brain.

sense organ A structure such as the eye, ear or nose that responds to external stimuli.

skull The bones of the head that protect the brain.

spinal canal The space inside the spine that contains the spinal cord.

spinal cord The bundle of nerve tissue inside the spinal canal.

spine The backbone.

thalamus A part of the brain involved with memories and emotions.

Further Information

Books

Body Books: Brain Box
by Anita Ganeri (Evans Brothers, 2002)

Body Science: Inside the Brain
by Rufus Bellamy (Franklin Watts, 2004)

DK Guide to the Human Body
(Dorling Kindersley, 2004)

*The Oxford Children's A to Z of the
Human Body*
by Bridget and Neil Ardley
(Oxford University Press, 2003)

Under the Microscope: Brain
by R. Walker (Franklin Watts, 2001)

*Usborne Internet-Linked Complete Book
of the Human Body*
by Anna Claybourne
(Usborne Publishing, 2003)

Websites

www.innerbody.com
Click on picture of nervous system

www.brainpop.com/health/index
Click on "brain"

Index